36640

South Worcestershire College
Learning Resource Centre
Malvern Campus
Albert Road North
Malvern, WR14 2YH

This book is to be returned
the last date star

36640

Ian Turpin

MAX ERNST

PHAIDON

The author and publishers would like to thank all those museum authorities and private owners who have kindly allowed works in their possession to be reproduced.

The photographs for Plates 8, 15, 17, 26 and 43 were taken by Jacqueline Hyde, Paris.

Phaidon Press Limited, Littlegate House, St Ebbe's Street, Oxford
Published in the United States of America by E. P. Dutton, New York

First published 1979

© 1979 by Phaidon Press Limited
Reproductions © 1979 by SPADEM, Paris

ISBN 0 7148 1995 6
Library of Congress Catalog Card Number: 79-50325

Printed in Great Britain by Morrison & Gibb Ltd, Edinburgh

MAX ERNST

Max Ernst was one of the most complex, as well as one of the most inventive, artists connected with the Dada and Surrealist movements. Associating with those groups because of their attitude of revolt – against the prevailing forms of social organization, politics and philosophy, as well as against the mainstream of contemporary art – Ernst not only made a number of important contributions to the development of Dada and Surrealism, but also elaborated aspects of Dada and Surrealist theory into a comprehensive approach to artistic creation.

The first point to note about Ernst's work is its enormous variety. Standing at the opposite pole to a painter (and fellow-Surrealist) like Magritte, who, with minor exceptions, never deviated from his mature style, Ernst created new techniques and new idioms with astonishing ease. He earned himself the title of 'the complete Surrealist' because of his mastery of both illusionism and abstraction – the dream pictures and automatic paintings which correspond to the two major aspects of Surrealist theory. If this diversity is reminiscent of Picasso, Ernst's art was very different in intention from that of the Cubist painter. Where Picasso claimed to *find* rather than to seek, Ernst's œuvre is characterized by an attitude of enquiry. It is this exploitation of many techniques and styles, in the service of a single aim, that provides the essential clue to Ernst's art. While Surrealist theory restricted the role of the Surrealists to that of 'simple recording machines' of the unconscious, Ernst refused to regard art as the mere record either of a dream or of the automatic activity of the hand. Rather, he saw his art as the *process* whereby both dreams and automatism are investigated, as well as the visible result of such investigations. In other words, it was not only a question of exploring the contents of the unconscious mind, but also of initiating a dialogue between the unconscious and the conscious. Many factors entered into this dialogue: unconsciousness seen as a property of mental phenomena on the one hand, and as the repository of universal human concerns (in Jung's sense) on the other; consciousness seen both as the organizing factor which gives ultimate meaning to experience, and as a fallible agent whose dominance produces a one-sided or incomplete picture of reality. Furthermore, Ernst believed that this dialogue between conscious and unconscious should take place on the canvas itself, in the very act of creation. To the extent that he regarded his art as a means of investigation rather than as an end to be savoured for itself, he was not deviating from the defined aims of Surrealism. On the other hand, his attempts to reconcile reason and intuition, intellect and inspiration, through the act of painting, forced him to focus his critical attention on his art in a way not attempted by any other Dada or Surrealist artist.

Ernst was born near Cologne in 1891. His childhood proved rich in incidents, both real and psychological, which later formed the substance of his art. Looming large in his memory was the figure of his father who, both as a deeply religious man responsible for Ernst's strict Catholic upbringing, and as a Sunday painter, provided a model against which he was to rebel. In spite of this autobiographical element, however, Ernst's art was not simply an attempt to exorcize phantoms from a mind prone to hallucination. A knowledge of the workings of the unconscious, gained through early reading of Freud, enabled Ernst not only to produce images which were consciously symbolic, but also to develop methodologies which would provoke psychic responses in the spectator analogous to those which originally prompted the works of art. To this extent, Ernst's approach differed from that of those Surrealists who stopped short at a simple acceptance of their dreams. As though foreseeing Freud's refusal to contribute to a Surrealist anthology of dreams on the grounds that such a collection would be meaningless without knowledge of the dreamer and the context of the dream, Ernst packed his pictures with references and allusions of a psychological, theological, scientific, historical, and even art-historical nature. Such an art is essentially literary. At the same time, Ernst's significance rests on the fact that he did not rely on illustration, but recreated his experiences through analogous artistic processes. This accounts for the relatedness of method, style and subject-matter across the wide spectrum of his œuvre.

Ernst's beginnings as an artist were marked by wide-ranging experiments in the field of modern painting. Chief amongst the early influences was Van Gogh, whose work was known to him well before the Cologne Sonderbund exhibition of modern art in 1912, which made Ernst commit himself to a career as a painter. This influence can be seen in a number of paintings dating from as early as 1909, which exhibit strong colour and vigorous brushwork. In 1911, just over a year after he entered Bonn University, where, largely to please his father, he had enrolled to read philosophy and psychology, Ernst met the Expressionist painter August Macke. Macke introduced Ernst to many other painters, including fellow-members of the 'Blue Rider' group and the French painter Robert Delaunay. Delaunay's 'Orphism' (an optical variant on Cubism), with its attendant colour symbolism, was an important influence on many German painters, including those of the Blue Rider. Ernst's response to this influence can be seen in *Flowers and Fish* (Plate 1), where it is filtered through the animism of Franz Marc. He painted the picture while serving as an artillery engineer with the German army during the First World War.

The influence of Expressionism on Ernst did not survive the First World War. As the leading avant-garde movement in Germany at the time, it was a prime target for the Dadaists' attack on Western culture. Yet Ernst was not drawn to Dada simply as a reaction against Expressionism, or for purely political reasons. The impetus came from interests which he had pursued during the pre-war period, and which began to play an important part in his art as the bankruptcy of Western civilization, and of the art it had spawned, became apparent to him. As a student of psychology Ernst had visited a local mental hospital, where paintings produced by the inmates had caught his imagination. The knowledge of psychology and of psychoanalytic theory that he gained during this period (particularly from reading Freud) enabled him to develop an understanding of the artistic products of the mentally ill, of children, and of primitive cultures, whose art was prized by the avant-garde for its formal characteristics.

The Dada revolt took a number of forms, from the overtly political to a faith in a new art as the only possible saviour of mankind. Although it was this latter aspect that attracted Ernst on his discharge from the army in 1917, his art, as it developed, was not informed by the simple optimism of Arp. Neither, however, did it bear much relation to the stringent iconoclasm of Dadaists like Marcel Duchamp.

Ernst's contribution to the Dada attack on both modernist art and accepted values in general was *collage* (Plates 2–5). First developed by the Cubist painters in 1912, collage had assumed important 'anti-art' connotations for the Dadaists, who made various uses of it, from the overtly political (*photomontage* in Berlin), to the essentially

4

formal (Schwitters's *Merz* collages in Hanover). Ernst lay somewhere between these two extremes. He regarded collage initially as a method of exploring the possibilities of representation outside the limitations of Cubist formalism. His concerns were not with abstract form, but with the strange juxtapositions which he was able to obtain by collaging parts of photographs and engravings. Ernst's discovery of this aspect of collage was prompted by the absurd combinations of objects in some scientific catalogues. These combinations, as he later described them, 'provoked a sudden intensification of the visionary faculties in me and brought forth an illusive succession of contradictory images . . . piling up on each other with the persistence and rapidity which are peculiar to love memories and visions of half sleep'. Ernst found that he could enhance the poetic effect of these juxtapositions by adding an odd line, an area of colour, or 'a landscape foreign to the represented objects'. These collages were not only or essentially anti-art gestures. Their dreamlike appearance also suggested the possibility of attacking contemporary values in general, particularly the reliance on reason. In this attack, Ernst posited the dream as the point at which the contents of the unconscious mind most easily enter consciousness. Ernst came to describe the additions he made to his collages as changing them into images which 'transformed into revealing dreams my most secret desires'.

Ernst's use of the dream as a matrix for the combination of unrelated objects had a number of precedents, the most important of which were the 'metaphysical' paintings of the Italian, Giorgio de Chirico, which Ernst first encountered through illustrations in 1919. These paintings by de Chirico exhibit, in varying combinations, conflicting perspectives, contradictory flat and modelled forms, strange lighting, and odd juxtapositions of unrelated objects, which combine to produce a consistent and convincing dreamlike effect. Although it was not until 1921 that Ernst fully accepted de Chirico's influence, the Italian painter did reveal to him the possibilities of a 'culture of systematic displacement and its effects', the immediate impact of which can be seen in a series of eight lithographs dated 1919, which Ernst entitled *Fiat Modes: Pereat Ars*.

In 1920, Ernst was joined in Cologne by Hans Arp, whom he had known for a brief period before the outbreak of war in 1914, and by the socialist activist Alfred Grünwald, alias Johannes Baargeld. Together they formed the Cologne Dada group, which over a period of little more than a year published a number of short-lived reviews and held two exhibitions. Cologne Dada was marked by the artistic bias of its activities. Although both exhibitions were more in the nature of Dada provocations than traditional art shows (at one, visitors were invited to destroy the exhibits with an axe, which was provided for the purpose), Ernst was at the same time working on a series of collages, which he showed in May 1921 at the 'Au Sans Pareil' gallery in Paris under the title 'Beyond Painting'. This exhibition, which had been organized by André Breton, the future leader of the Surrealist group, is evidence of the close contact with Paris which was a distinguishing characteristic of Dada in Cologne. The collages which Ernst exhibited (Plates 3–5) reveal a variety of arrangements, from the simple modification of a single image, to the creation of composite creatures from parts of objects drawn from similar sources. These objects are sometimes inconsistently modelled; sometimes they are placed in a space which contradicts either their modelling or their perspectival arrangement; sometimes they are thrust towards their picture-plane in violent foreshortening, which increases their psychological impact. As well as recalling de Chirico, these collages also reveal the influence of the mechanistic imagery of Ernst's fellow-Dadaists Duchamp and Picabia. The close link between the Dada poets and painters is reflected in the importance which Ernst attached to the titles of his collages. Clearly composed on the same principle as the images, he designated the titles themselves 'verbal collages'. Frequently long and poetically written, often in several languages, on the works themselves, their distortion of commonsense reality parallels that of the images, to which they bear a reciprocal relation as both inspiration and amplification. This practice coincided with his enthusiastic reading of Novalis and Hölderlin. Ernst's experiments with word-image combinations – which were to influence the development of *peinture-poésie*, which the Surrealists opposed to the pure abstraction of the avant-garde – came to a head in a series of *Picture-Poems* dating from 1923–4 (Plate 16). Here the words not only react with the image, they form part of the very structure of the composition.

The rapturous reception which Ernst's collages received when they were exhibited in Paris in 1921 presaged the contribution he was to make not only in helping Breton define Surrealism in theory, but also in providing a model for those painters who were to respond to Breton's call for dream description. During the period between his Paris exhibition and Breton's first *Manifesto of Surrealism* (1924), the so-called '*époque floue*', Ernst returned to canvas and painted a series of works in which he combined his collage preoccupations with devices derived from de Chirico, though interpreted in more personal terms (Plates 6–10 and 13).

In *The Teetering Woman* (Plate 10), de Chirico's stage setting, here featuring classical pillars, supports a barely modelled, collage-like machine image. Other paintings in the series exhibit such collage-derived features as hybrid creatures and conflicting perspectives, but with a greater emphasis on confrontations between unrelated objects within an irrational context. Both *Celebes* (Plate 6) and *Woman, Old Man & Flower* (Plate 9) use heterogeneous creatures as the main protagonists. In the former painting an imposing figure, based on Sudanese corn bins and resembling a vacuum cleaner, confronts a headless, gloved, classical nude and a strange pillar reminiscent of the occupants of *The Hat Makes the Man* (Plate 4). The body of the old man in the latter picture consists of a broken flowerpot, while the woman's head is a fan, and her body pierced metal sheeting. In *Oedipus Rex* (Plate 8) the modelling of the pierced hand, which emerges through a window clutching a walnut, contradicts that of the birds' heads, which appear curiously flat in comparison. The contradictory viewpoints from which the birds' heads and the enclosing fence are seen augment the effect of the perspectives in the buildings in creating an indecipherable space. In a number of these paintings, objects float through the sky, to varying effect. In *Oedipus Rex* the unexceptional nature of the hot air balloon contrasts with the strange inhabitants of the earth below. In *Celebes* the sky is confused with the sea to the extent of supporting a number of fish. Despite the fact that the subject-matter of these 1921–4 paintings frequently presupposes a knowledge of Freudian theory, the actual psychological element is largely personal. This is seen most clearly by comparing *Pietà, or Revolution by Night* (Plate 7) with *At the First Clear Word* (Plate 12). In the latter picture the sexual theme is made explicit in the identification of the outstretched fingers of the hand with the lower female torso. In the former, the paternal figure supporting the barely sketched younger one is undoubtedly Ernst's father, who painted many religious pictures, in at least one of which the face of the infant Jesus is modelled on that of the young Max Ernst. Childhood experience, this time of terror, appears in *Two Children are Threatened by a Nightingale* (Plate 13). This work is remarkable for its extension of the use made in the collages of lithographed and photographed images as a ready-made reality to the incorporation of wooden constructions.

Here the psychic dislocation does not result so much from a combination of style and content as from a clash between the two. A man runs (or perhaps falls, a feeling common in dreams) across the roof of a wooden house towards a real alarm bell, while a girl pursues a nightingale (the shyest of birds) which has just felled her sister, against a background in vertiginous perspective, which features a triumphal arch at the far end and a wooden gate swinging on real hinges at the near. Although *Men Shall Know Nothing of This* (Plate 11) depends for its effect, like the other paintings in the series, on the shock of recognition as we piece together the various elements, it also contains a significant illustrative aspect which makes reference to many sources: scientific, psychoanalytical, astrological, and occult. On the back of the painting Ernst provided an interpretation in the form of a poem, which ends: 'The moon runs quickly through its phases and eclipses. This picture is curious in its symmetry. The two sexes are in equilibrium.'

In 1922, the year which saw Breton's first tentative definition of Surrealism as 'a certain psychic automatism that corresponds rather closely to the state of dreaming', Ernst entered illegally into France, to stay at the home of the poet Paul Eluard. In 1924 he accompanied Eluard and his wife on a trip to the Far East. After a few months he returned to Paris, to a group that was avidly discussing Breton's 'First Manifesto', which had been published during Ernst's absence. Breton's document is remarkable as a codification of ideas which had been present in Dada, particularly concerning automatism and chance, and a justification for their extension based on Freudian psychology.

Ernst's reaction was to change both the basis and the style of his painting, and he did so under the impetus of a discovery which he related to Breton's automatism, but which derived in the first place from his own childhood memories. This discovery was *frottage*. As Ernst described it, the deeply indented grooves of a wooden floor which he was examining one day reminded him of a childhood memory of false mahogany panelling, which had, at the time, brought to mind associations of organic forms. Placing paper randomly over the floorboards and rubbing with a pencil on the back, Ernst was surprised by the way in which, as he put it, 'the drawings thus obtained steadily lose . . . the character of the material studied – wood – and assume the aspect of unbelievably clear images of a kind able to reveal the first cause of the obsession.'

Thirty-four frottages were published in Paris in 1926, under the title *Histoire naturelle* (Plate 14). These added to the dreamlike combination of objects in the Dada collages a similar confrontation between textures. These textures were combined into rubbings which give the appearance of having emerged from the subconscious bearing the imprint of some subliminal obsession. Some of these frottages remain relatively close to their sources. In one, a few floorboards take on the impression of a wooden fence. In others, such as the one illustrated here, the sources are all but inde-cipherable. These frottages, with their mysterious figures and subtle tonality, are amongst the most exquisite works of graphic art produced this century. Notwithstand-ing this, Ernst stressed the links between frottage and automatism. Belying the adroitness that undoubtedly went into their production, he wrote that the role of the artist had been reduced to that of 'spectator . . . at the birth of his work', which was thereby put beyond those controls normally associated with art: reason, taste, morality.

The period immediately following the discovery of frottage was a very productive one for Ernst. Under the influence of fellow-Surrealist painter Miró, Ernst adapted the process of frottage to oil painting. The new process was known as *grattage*. It consisted of scraping wet paint from unstretched canvas which was draped over objects and surfaces. The resulting textures were partially elaborated with a brush amongst the several layers of the painted surface which were revealed. The adaptation of frottage to oil-paint is well illustrated in *Two Sisters* (Plate 20), where Ernst not only stuck fairly close to the sources of the textures, and even imitated with black paint the effect of pencil frottage, but also echoed the subtle tonality of the *Histoire naturelle* series in pastel colouring.

In *To the 100,000 Doves* (Plate 18) the birds' heads, brushed in amongst the dense texturing, suggest a vast flock. Here, the shallow space of the *Histoire naturelle* frottages is completely flattened out. The figurative elements lack modelling, and emerge from the background to form a grid reminiscent of those resulting from the disintegration of the visible world in Analytic Cubism.

The *Forest* series of pictures refer directly to Ernst's childhood, as well as to the work of earlier German painters. Ernst's early feelings towards forests were equivocal. They were delightful and oppressive places at the same time, offering both the freedom of the open air and, in their depths, an atmosphere of entombment. These feelings were expressed with powerful simplicity in *The Great Forest* (Plate 25). The forest, which in the series as a whole can be read either as trees or as rocky crags, has no depth to it; it is placed close to the picture-plane and takes on the appearance of a stage-flat. Behind it is a brushed-in illusionistic sky, containing a sun- or moon-like ring which emits an eerie light. The combination of illusionism and artifice creates an unsettling scene which leads us to question how much of what we see is really there, outside us, and how much we create for ourselves. Ernst's approach to the tradition of forest painting in Germany reflected the influence of the Romantics' 'emotion in the face of nature'. Ernst himself referred to Caspar David Friedrich's exhortation to painters to close their physical eyes in order to see with the 'spiritual eye'. Ernst's spiritual vision interpreted the forest in terms of both personal fantasy and the universal collective unconscious. Some of the forests contain trapped birds, which increases the sense of foreboding and recalls both the darker side of German fairytales (which again Ernst remembered from his childhood) and the extravagant horror of eighteenth-century Gothic novels, which the Surrealists so prized.

The textures of the *Horde* series (Plate 24) were created by using different thicknesses of rope, from whose coils emerge threatening anthropomorphs. As in the *Forest* series, the background is brushed in, though here it plays a more purely plastic role, locking the horde to the picture-plane. The fact that the group fills the picture-space renders *The Horde* less subtly menacing and more purely aggressive than the *Forests*. Whereas the latter are recognizable dream landscapes, *The Horde* works as a metaphor for the darker side of the unconscious.

A variant on the rope grattage process was responsible for *One Night of Love* (Plate 26), a similarly powerful but richer and more complex work than *The Horde*. Ernst dropped different thicknesses of paint-soaked rope onto the canvas, and from the linear pattern thus formed he developed a horned male creature, a female figure, and various animal forms. The male, his dark colouring and bared teeth combining into a threatening presence, appears to be moulding the female and animal forms, which, with the exception of the bird in the male's hands, are the same colour as the surface on which they rest, and rendered insubstantial in comparison with the male. The generalized violence of *The Horde* is here made more specific, and may refer, given Ernst's identification with birds (see below), to the moment of his own conception. The anatomical distortions, resulting partly from Ernst's painting method, also derive from Miró, Picasso's monumental groups of the 1920s, and the conflicting perspectives of de Chirico. This reference to the work of other painters also provides a clue to the sand-textured surface of *One Night of Love*, which contrasts with the dryness of many of Ernst's earlier anti-art paintings.

On a much simpler and more purely decorative level, Ernst painted a series of works around 1927 known as the *Snow Flowers* (Plate 22). Here, forms reminiscent of flowers and shells, created by the grattage process, are set off against flatly painted backgrounds, some of which, as here, are given a spatial dimension through the use of different coloured areas.

The bird that appears caged in *Snow Flowers* was a symbol of which Ernst had made ample use in his work from an early stage (see Plates 5, 8, 13, 14, 18, 25, and 26). In the mid-1920s this interest came to the fore, and emerged as an obsession with one creature in particular: 'Loplop, the Superior of the Birds'. This obsession derived from a childhood incident in which the death of a pet cockatoo coincided with the birth of a sister. As Ernst described it, in the third person: 'In his imagination he connected both events and charged the baby with the extinction of the bird's life. . . . A dangerous confusion between birds and humans became encrusted in his mind.' There were undoubtedly other sources for Loplop; for example, birds play an important role in German mythology. There are also references to birds in the writings of Freud. One such credits Leonardo da Vinci with a vulture fixation, based on the bird's disguised appearance in the painting *The Virgin and Child with St Anne* (Louvre). In the earlier paintings dealing with this obsession the birds are often trapped, for example in a forest (Plate 25), or in a cage (Plate 22). In 1927, however, Loplop emerged victorious, in a painting which prefigured Ernst's return, in the 1930s, to a more literal realism. *Monument to the Birds* (Plate 17), a reference to the Renaissance tradition of Assumption pictures, is painted in the dry manner which characterizes the works of the early 1920s inspired by de Chirico (Plates 6–10 and 13). Ernst rarely touched on religious themes. As a piece of Dada provocation he had painted a sacrilegious work entitled *The Virgin Mary Beating the Infant Jesus* (1923), and in 1931 Loplop emerged as *Chaste Joseph*, a reference to Ernst Senior, the painter of religious themes and father of a large family. The last year of the decade saw a series of paintings generically entitled *On the Inside of Sight* (Plate 21), in which bird-forms inhabit rounded or egg shapes in a confusion between inner and outer, unconscious and conscious. Loplop also made numerous appearances in the guise of a master of ceremonies. In a number of oil paintings he is presenting another picture, which forms his body. These pictures within pictures are always variations on works by Ernst. Elsewhere he takes on a more anthropomorphic appearance. In a low relief, *Loplop Presents a Young Girl*, the bird holds a frame containing a number of collage objects, including the girl's profile.

During the 1930s Ernst approached collage from two angles. He took as his subject the complex interplay between various approaches to representation (Plates 23 and 28) and underlying assumptions both about the nature of reality and about our perception of it. The antagonism between unconscious and conscious response, which forms the basis of the mystery of *Loplop Presents* (Plate 28), exists as a conflict between two different styles: the flat, decorative qualities of the marbled paper and ink-blotter, and the illusionism of the art-manual drawings, all of which are arranged in an almost Cubist manner. Loplop, in the form of an outline drawing, arbitrates between the two styles: in effect, he attempts to reintegrate the human personality.

Ernst's mastery of collage was put to its most effective use in the 1930s in another of his discoveries, the collage novel (Plates 15 and 29). These 'novels' consist of a series of collages based on nineteenth-century book illustrations, which Ernst cut up and reassembled. The relationship between the collage novels and those whose illustrations they use is a complex one. Not only did the original novels provide Ernst with subject-matter through their illustrations, which served as his source material; they also represented an attitude whose satirization is Ernst's real theme. Taking as his point of departure Breton's attack on the nineteenth-century novel as an example of the despised 'realistic attitude', with its underpinning of reason and logic, Ernst presents us with unusual juxtapositions which invert the original meaning of their source. Through small changes which bring about confrontations between objects and contexts, Ernst turned what had been simple illustrations into explicit condemnations of Victorian society. His main themes were religious bigotry and sexual repression, which, after Freud, were held responsible for all manner of ills, both psychological and physical. Furthermore, the very form of the collage novels involved an implicit criticism of the society which found expression in the novel form, since they lack a story which unfolds towards a dénouement, and consist instead of a series of episodes only loosely related and having no ending.

The first of these collage novels was published in 1929. Its title, *La Femme 100 têtes* (Plate 15), is a pun on the French words *cent* (a hundred) and *sans* (without), so that the woman is simultaneously headless and blessed with more than her fair share of heads. Each collage has a caption, which plays a role similar to that of the titles of the Dada collages, often exhibiting a strong element of Surrealist 'black humour'. The brief title *Yachting* which accompanies the collage illustrated evokes perfectly the idyllic situation which will be shattered irrevocably when the sailor turns round to be confronted by the huge dismembered limbs lying on the bench beside him.

In 1934 Ernst published *Une Semaine de bonté* which was subtitled *Les Sept éléments capitaux* (Plate 29). Appearing as five separate booklets, *Une Semaine de bonté* gives us one 'deadly element', and an example of that element, for each day of the week. The collage illustrated comes from 'Wednesday's Book'. Its element is 'blood' (of the traditional four elements, Ernst retained only fire and water) and its example is 'Oedipus', who broke laws regarding sexual relations with blood relatives, and with whom the Sphinx of the illustration is associated. The action of *Une Semaine de bonté* is much more dramatic, not to say theatrical, than that of *La Femme 100 têtes*. This possibly reflects the deepening gloom of the European political situation as much as the crisis which occurred in Ernst's art (as it did in much Surrealist as well as avant-garde painting) in the 1930s. The characters of *Une Semaine de bonté* are in general both closer to the picture-plane and larger in relation to the surrounding space than those of the earlier novel. There is consequently a feeling not so much of a conflict between conscious and unconscious, as of a direct assault by the latter on the former.

The 1930s saw a significant change both in Ernst's attitude towards Surrealism and in his approach to artistic problems. Surrealist painting of the period was dominated by the illusionism of Dali, Magritte and Tanguy, while the abstractionists Masson and Miró, as well as Ernst himself, suffered a failing inventiveness. The deepening gloom apparent in much Surrealist painting of the 1930s mirrored the worsening political and economic situation in Europe, although (reflecting Breton's refusal to commit Surrealism as a propaganda machine for the left) the Surrealist painters did not comment directly upon it. The only exception to this was Ernst, who, through the use of allegory and symbol, focused his attention on those darker aspects of man's personality which were coming to the fore. This new approach consisted of a novel emphasis on what Ernst regarded as the failure of reconciliation between conscious and unconscious, reason and intuition, and the practical results of this failure.

During the 1930s Ernst relied on styles and methods he had invented in the 1920s. He alternated between flat patterning derived from his frottage and grattage works (Plates 27 and 31) and sculptural illusion which harked back to the period of the early 1920s inspired by de Chirico (Plates 30 and 32–4). At the same time, his work possessed a confidence which belied both his financial situation, which was never very stable, and his position as a member of the Surrealist group, which deteriorated after his temporary expulsion, along with Miró, in 1926, for designing sets for a Diaghilev ballet.

In the *Garden Aeroplane-Trap* series (Plate 30) poisonous plants lurk within a series of walled areas to trap and destroy passing planes. Ernst owned a nineteenth-century manual of bird-trapping methods, and in turning from Loplop to man-made flyers he was making a comment on the decreasing political and intellectual liberty in Europe at the time. The cool colour and dry precision of the brushwork accentuate rather than diminish the horror of the scene. The conventional perspective of the *Garden Aeroplane-Traps* attests to the influence of the illusionistic Surrealists on Ernst. There is, however, nothing in their work quite so coolly fantastic as these natural machines of destruction.

The ramparts of the *Garden Aeroplane-Traps* developed into complete fortresses in a series of paintings of *Whole Cities* (Plate 31). These are basically variations on the *Forest* pictures of the later 1920s (Plate 25). Similarly created through the grattage process, they consist either of flat patterning close up to the picture-plane, or an illusion of shallow depth, as in the one illustrated here. A flat disc sun casts a menacing light over most of the cities in the series, and in some cases illuminates a carnivorous jungle in the foreground, whose threatening presence is made more sinister because its illusionistic style contrasts with the flatness of the city itself. The *Whole City* series can be seen as a metaphor for the destruction of man's rational constructions by the dark forces of the unconscious mind, when those forces remain repressed.

The spiky vegetation which creeps menacingly upwards in *The Whole City* developed into a lush, though no less dangerous, forest in a series painted in the years 1936–8, of which *Joie de Vivre* (Plate 32) is an example. In this series, the contrast between the luxuriance of the vegetation and Ernst's dry painting manner offers a clue to the picture's theme. The vegetation does not represent the richness of life, but its dangers, for it conceals predatory animals—and is even confused with them at points. Outwardly reminiscent of the mysterious but always friendly jungles of the 'Douanier' Rousseau, whose work was greatly admired by the Surrealists, Ernst's jungles spawn monsters and exude an air of entrapment. His rejection of the Surrealist 'resolution' of dream and reality is here extended to the Romantic notion of a harmony between man and nature. The forest, which spelt freedom as well as confinement to the young Ernst, has come to offer only death.

The delight in conjuring up monsters with which to mock man's reliance on his rational powers, which *Joie de Vivre* evinces, became more explicit in a number of paintings which Ernst made towards the end of the 1930s, and of which *The Angel of Hearth and Home* (Plate 33) and *The Robing of the Bride* (Plate 34) are good examples. Both paintings possess a dreamlike clarity; yet where in earlier paintings the combination of rationally unrelated objects was aimed at providing that 'spark' which would illuminate the depths of the unconscious, the dream here has produced monsters whose threat is as much physical as psychic. The former work was painted after the defeat of the Republicans in the Spanish Civil War, and represents a rare reference by Ernst to a specific political event. For a brief period the painting bore the ironic title *Triumph of Surrealism*, as though Ernst had despaired even of the movement's aims. The year following its completion saw Ernst's final break with Surrealism, over Breton's rupture with Paul Eluard, who had been Ernst's lifelong friend. Although Ernst had put his name to a number of Surrealist documents, he had always maintained a certain distance from the group, which he had always regarded as a prerequisite of creative freedom.

Perhaps the finest work which Ernst produced during the 1930s was a series featuring images of a simultaneously psychological and sexual nature. *Blind Swimmer* (Plate 27) represents a culmination of Ernst's interest in the relationship between sexual and psychological repression. The seed forcing its way along the channels, which derive formally from his earlier wood frottages, represents at one and the same time the male seed, the repressed contents of the unconscious, and the creative impulse, all seeking an outlet.

On the outbreak of war in 1939 Ernst was interned by the French authorities as an enemy alien. During this internment he met fellow-Surrealist Hans Bellmer, and together they experimented with a technique of automatic painting which had first been used by Oscar Dominguez in 1935. The 'decalcomania' technique, which consists of sandwiching ink between layers of paper, had been received with enthusiasm by the Surrealist group, particularly the poets. With little skill they were able to achieve interesting results susceptible to multiple interpretation in the manner of Rorschach inkblots. It was left to Ernst, however, to apply the decalcomania technique to oil-paint and canvas (Plates 35–7 and 39). In so doing he developed the iconographic possibilities of his earlier jungle pictures and produced some of the most penetrating comments on contemporary society in the whole of modern art.

As with the earlier grattage process (Plates 18–20, 22, 24–6), Ernst worked up suggestions provided by the initial automatic sandwiching, using a brush, and finally painted in a background. However, the decalcomania paintings differ from the earlier examples of developed automatism in a number of important respects. Firstly, the working-up in, for example, *Napoleon in the Wilderness* (Plate 35), consists of the addition of conventionally illusionistic areas, which contrast with the original paintwork. This juxtaposition of different styles and methods creates an atmosphere of disjointedness, as in dreams, and relates the painting to the collage process of odd combinations. In other paintings of the series (for example, Plate 36) the clash is less acute because the decalcomania areas take on a distinctly *trompe-l'oeil* character, reminiscent of the work of Gustave Moreau. These paintings reveal Ernst's ability to conjure the richness of reality from the very stuff of the paint itself. Secondly, the implications of the relationship between foreground and background differ between the two methods. In the grattage works (see Plates 25 and 31) the contrast between the flat patterning of the main subject and the view back into infinite space suggests the distance between two realities: Freud's 'pleasure' and 'reality' principles. This is not the case in the decalcomania pictures, where the *trompe-l'oeil* nature of the automatic passages relates them to the background, which acts as an impassive backdrop to the foreground action.

The most imposing painting of the series is undoubtedly *Europe After the Rain II*

(Plate 36), which Ernst began in France and completed in America after a long and perilous flight. Here the decalcomania technique has produced a spongy, rotting landscape redolent of decay. As an indictment of war it works much more effectively than the earlier *Angel of Hearth and Home* (Plate 33). Animal, vegetable and mineral forms simultaneously emerge from and sink back into the substance of the paint.

The Temptation of St Antony (Plate 39) exhibits more brushwork than other paintings in the series, and harks back more directly to the jungle pictures of the 1930s (see Plate 32). In the period after about 1935, Ernst turned increasingly to the traditional Germanic interest in forests and in monsters to express his feelings about the political developments which were symptomatic of the psychological development of modern European man. Both in its confusion of plant and animal forms and in its dark pessimism, *The Temptation of St Antony* is reminiscent of the visions of such German painters as Schongauer and Grünewald.

In other pictures of the period Ernst restated some of his earlier concerns, for example *peinture-poésie* (Plate 38), and a more orthodox Surrealist dream atmosphere. In another major work dating from Ernst's stay in America, *Vox Angelica* (Plate 37), he recapitulated in a systematic manner the various styles and techniques which he had incorporated in his art over the previous quarter-century. This painting is divided into a series of rectangular areas by framelike horizontals and verticals. It features, amongst other things, passages of decalcomania, frottage, grattage, and 1930s forestation, as well as imprisoned birds and mathematical instruments. Ernst wrote of the painting that it was an 'autobiographical account, in episodes of dream and reality, of his peregrinations from one country to another'. His actual physical moves are represented by the Eiffel Tower and the Empire State Building.

An area towards the top right-hand corner of *Vox Angelica* contains a passage in which Ernst referred to the last technical innovation of his career. 'Oscillation', as this method was known, was an automatic technique in which liquid paint was dripped from a small hole in the bottom of a tin can, which was swung randomly from the end of a piece of string over a canvas laid horizontally on the floor. It was, however, used for only a few paintings (Plate 42), which suggests that Ernst found it insufficiently flexible for his expressive needs.

The increasing importance of sculptural illusion in Surrealist art during the 1930s was reflected in a corresponding interest shown by the group in actual objects. After Breton's call for the manufacture of irrational objects from dreams, the Surrealist object took on an importance as the concrete materialization of secret desires.

This move was reflected in Ernst's art by an interest in sculpture, which emerged in 1934. Before that time, his investigations into the third dimension had been few. From his Dada days little remains but a wood relief entitled *Fruit of a Long Experience*. This work, which is close to the collage reliefs of fellow-Dadaist Kurt Schwitters, was more a Dada protest against the traditional materials of paint and canvas than a real attempt to move out of two dimensions. Ernst's interest in sculpture was stimulated by a visit he made to Switzerland in the summer of 1934, where he stayed with the sculptor Giacometti. Using Giacometti's tools, he modelled in low relief some stones which the two found in a local riverbed. On his return to Paris he began working in plaster. He combined casts of everyday objects, on the collage principle, to create strange creatures whose humour contrasts with the darker aspects of his contemporary paintings. Pieces such as *Head-Bird* (Plate 40) reflect an awareness of primitive art more than of modern sculpture. Indeed, Ernst's ignorance of the work of contemporary sculptors seems to have lent his efforts a freshness which was conspicuously lacking in theirs during the 1930s. Ernst let sculpture drop after 1935 and did not take it up again until 1944, when he was living on Long Island. Here he began a series on the theme of chess. The most imposing of these, *The King Playing with the Queen* (Plate 41), derives both from Giacometti's tabletop sculptures of the early 1930s and from certain of Ernst's own paintings, particularly *One Night of Love* (Plate 26).

In 1946 Ernst moved to Arizona. His experience of the landscape and of the light there proved decisive in determining the direction his art took from then on until his death. *Coloradeau of Medusa* (Plate 45), which was inspired by a visit to the Colorado River, has the appearance of rock strata seen through a heat haze. The interpenetrating layers of colour suggest a mindscape in which the relationship between conscious and unconscious levels has become confused.

On his return to Europe in 1953 Ernst settled in Paris, but made an almost immediate visit to Cologne. This trip resulted in *Old Father Rhine* (Plate 44), a tribute to the river. As a more abstract work than others in which the decalcomania technique had been employed, *Old Father Rhine* presaged Ernst's increasing response to the importance of colour and form in French painting, which emerged fully in such pictures as *The World of the Naïve* (Plate 47) and *The Marriage of Heaven and Earth* (Plate 48). This new interest in light and colour sustained him after the effective demise of Surrealism, which never reasserted itself after the war. Throughout his mature career colour had played a largely secondary role; being based on such techniques as photographic collage and pencil frottage, his art had responded to treatment in terms of light and dark.

Ernst continued to paint, largely in this light-hearted manner, but with occasional reversions (of a semi-serious nature) back to styles and methods of his Dada and Surrealist days, amidst growing acclaim, until his death in 1976. Numerous retrospective exhibitions of his work were held, one even in his home town, and in 1954 he was awarded the Grand Prize for painting at the Venice Biennale.

The variety and richness of Ernst's œuvre makes him one of the most satisfying of twentiety-century artists. His genius lay in devising many and varied techniques for the treatment of his subject. His strength lay in refusing to illustrate an *a priori* theory but using his art as a tool of investigation. If he continues to engage our attention, it is because, as he put it himself: 'in yielding quite naturally to the vocation of pushing back appearances and upsetting the relations of "realities" [we have helped] to hasten the general crisis of consciousness due in our time.'

Outline Biography

1891	Born in Brühl, near Cologne, son of a teacher and amateur painter.
1909–12	Studies philosophy, psychology and art history at Bonn University. In 1911 joins August Macke's *Rheinische Expressionisten* group.
1914–17	Serves as an artillery engineer in the German army. Paints in his spare time. Exhibits with the Zurich Dadaists in 1917.
1920	Founds the Cologne Dada group, with Arp and Baargeld. Makes his first collages. Makes contact with the Paris Dadaists.
1922	Settles illegally in France, at the home of Eluard.
1924	After a short trip to the Far East with the Eluards, returns to Paris and associates with the Surrealist group.
1925	Develops frottage. Contributes to the first Surrealist group exhibition.
1929	Publishes his first collage novel.
1934	Spends the summer in Switzerland with Giacometti, and makes his first serious sculpture.
1938	Leaves the Surrealist group over Breton's call to ostracize Eluard. Moves to St-Martin-d'Ardèche.
1939	On the outbreak of war is interned as an enemy alien, during which time he uses the decalcomania technique with oil paint. After release, re-internment, and escape (in 1940, shortly before a final release is ordered), he makes his way, via Spain, to New York, where he arrives on 14 July 1941.
1946–52	Lives in Arizona. In 1949 returns to Paris but is forced back to America by financial difficulties.
1953	Returns finally to France, and sets up studio in Paris. Visits Cologne for the first time in twenty-five years.
1954	Wins the Grand Prize for painting at the Venice Biennale.
1955	Settles at Huismes (Loire).
1958	Takes French citizenship.
1964	Moves to Seillans.
1976	Dies, on 1 April.

Select Bibliography

COLLAGE NOVELS, ETC., BY THE ARTIST

Fiat Modes, Pereat Ars. Cologne, Schlömilch Verlag, 1919.

Les Malheurs des Immortels (with Paul Eluard). Paris, Librarie Six, 1922.

Histoire naturelle. Paris, Eds. Jeanne Bucher, 1926.

La Femme 100 têtes. Paris, Eds. du Carrefour, 1929.

Rêve d'une petite fille qui voulut entrer au Carmel. Paris, Eds. du Carrefour, 1930.

Une Semaine de bonté ou Les Sept éléments capitaux. Paris, Eds. Jeanne Bucher, 1934; New York, Dover Publications, 1976.

A L'Intérieur de la vue. 8 poèmes visibles (with Paul Eluard). Paris, Seghers, 1947.

Sept Microbes vus à travers un tempérament. Paris, Eds. Cercle des Arts, 1953.

Maximiliana ou L'Exercice illégal de l'Astronomie. Paris, Le Degré Quarante-et-un, 1964.

Ernst, M., *Beyond Painting and Other Writings by the Artist and his Friends* (The Documents of Modern Art). New York, Wittenborn, Schultz, 1948.

Ernst, M., 'An Informal Life of M.E.', in *Max Ernst*. New York, The Museum of Modern Art, 1961 (exhibition catalogue).

Ernst, M., *Ecritures*. Paris, Gallimard, 1970.

Waldberg, P., *Max Ernst*. Paris, Pauvert, 1958.

Russell, J., *Max Ernst: Life and Work*. London, Thames and Hudson, 1967.

Spies, W., *Max Ernst: Frottages*. London, Thames and Hudson, 1969.

Schneede, U., *The Essential Max Ernst*. London, Thames and Hudson, 1972.

New York, The Solomon R. Guggenheim Museum, *Max Ernst: a Retrospective*, 1975 (exhibition catalogue).

Paris, Grand Palais des Champs-Elysées, *Max Ernst*, 1975 (exhibition catalogue).

Quinn, E., *Max Ernst*. London, Thames and Hudson, 1977.

List of Plates

1. *Flowers and Fish*. 1916. U.S.A., private collection

2. *Undulating Katharine*. 1920. London, private collection

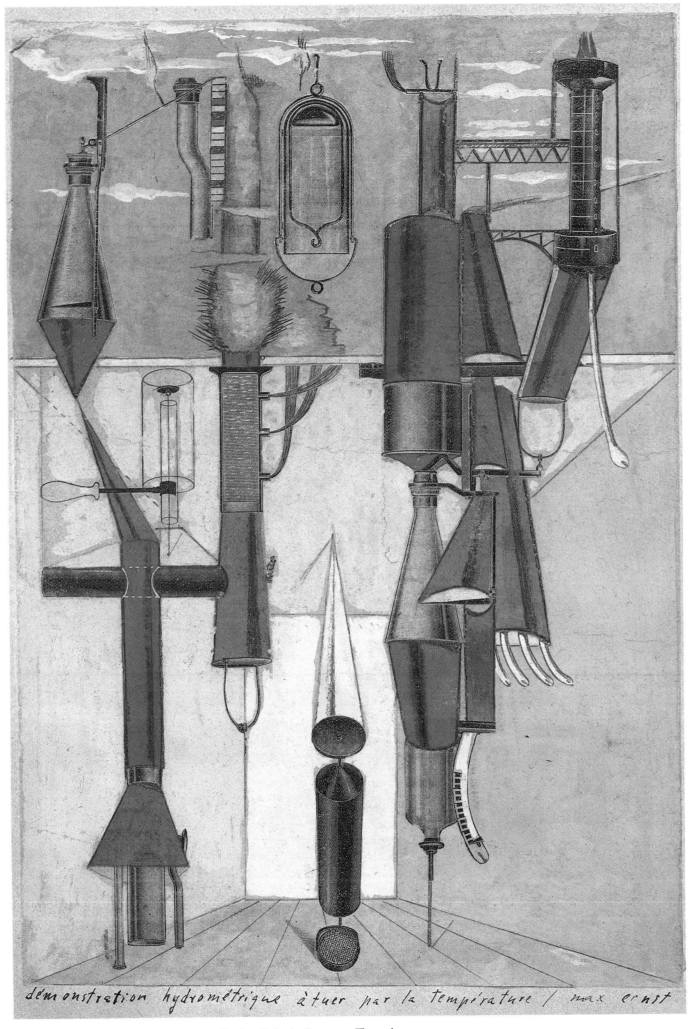

démonstration hydrométrique à tuer par la température / max ernst

3. *Hydrometric Demonstration.* 1920. Paris, Galerie Jacques Tronche

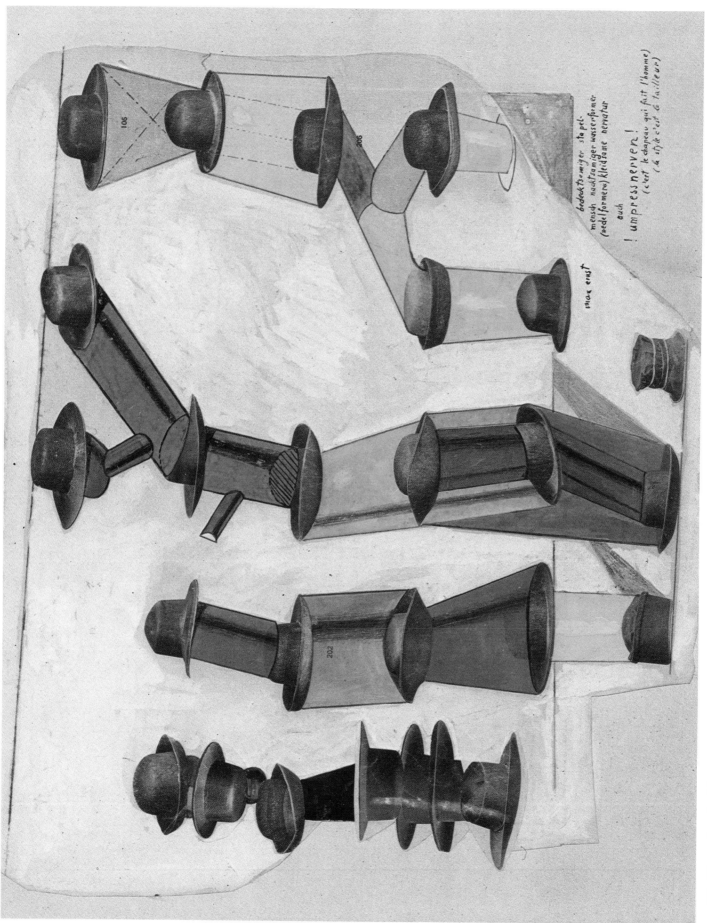

4. *The Hat makes the Man.* 1920. New York, Museum of Modern Art

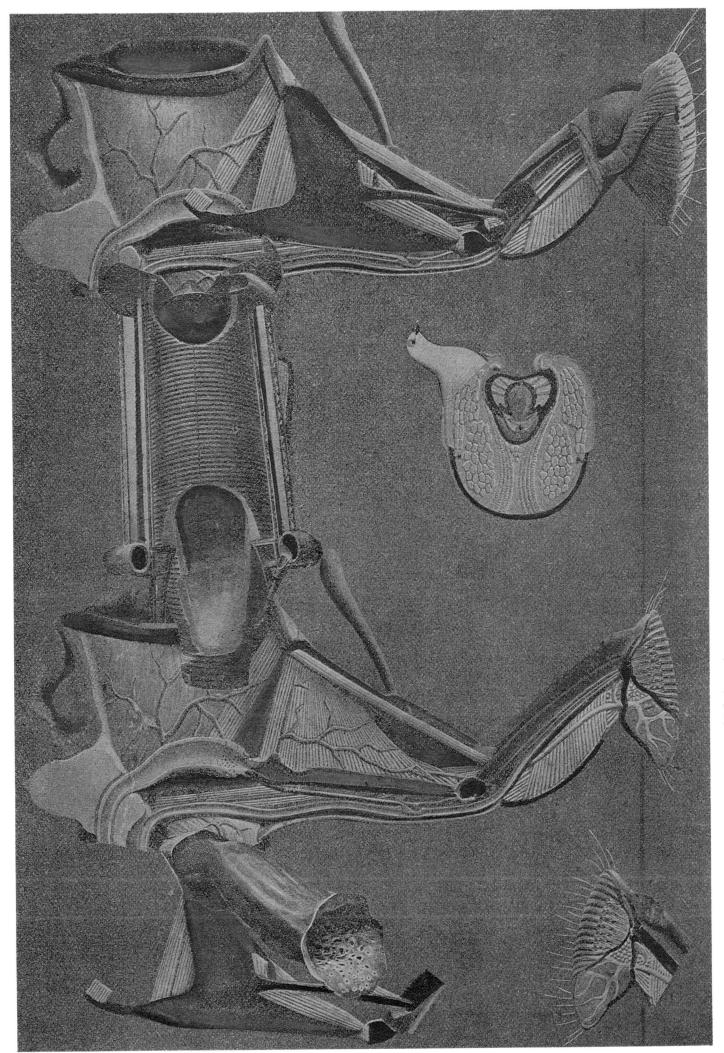

5. *The Horse, He's Sick.* 1920. New York, Museum of Modern Art

6. *Celebes*. 1921. London, Tate Gallery

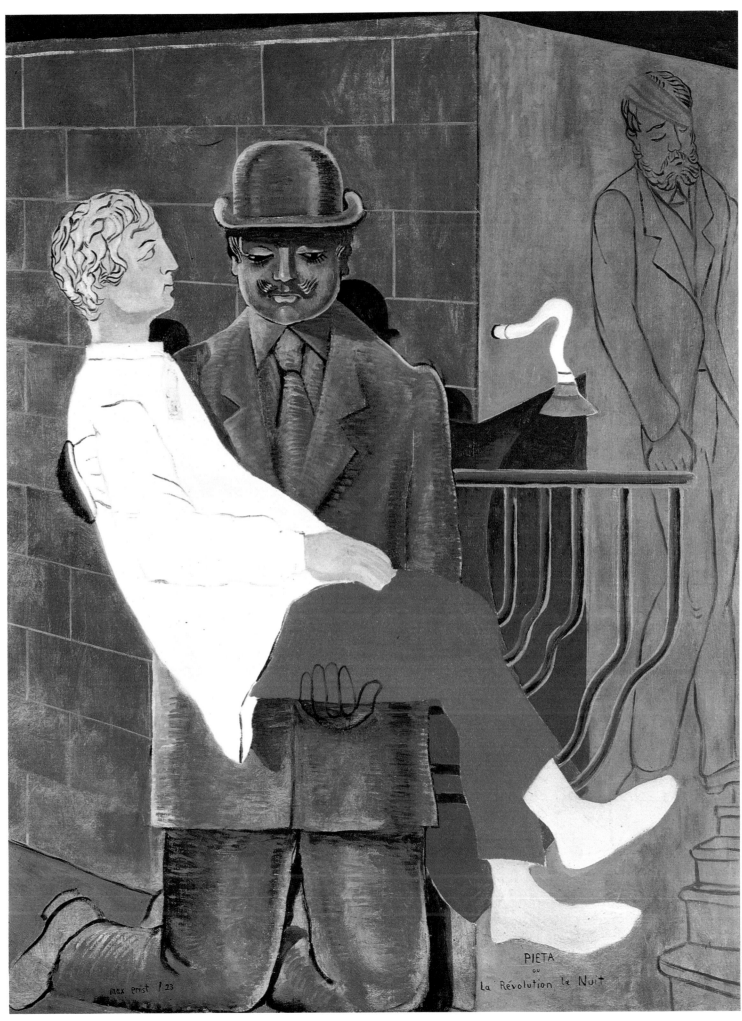

7. *Pietà, or Revolution by Night.* 1923. Turin, private collection

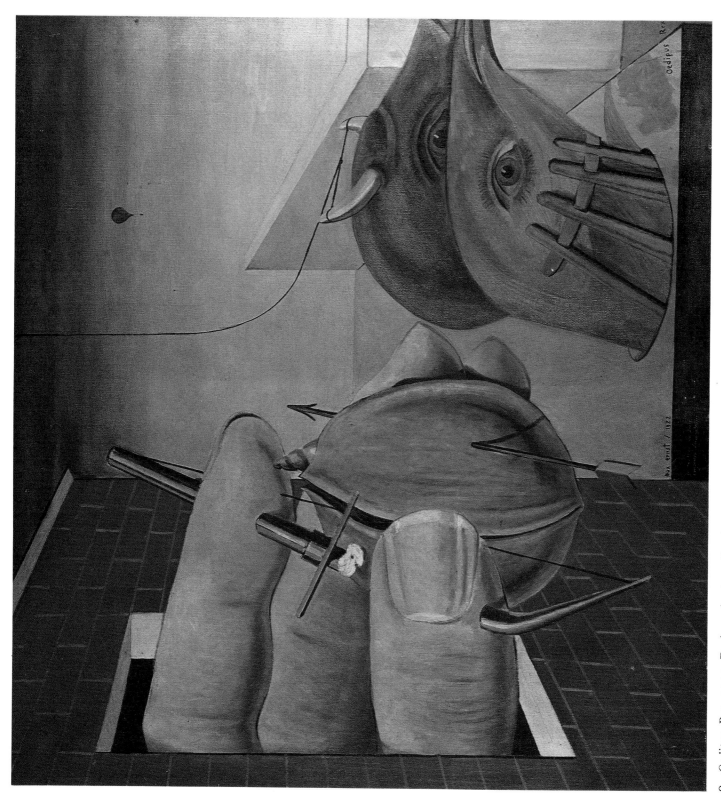

8. *Oedipus Rex.* 1922. Paris, private collection

9. *Woman, Old Man & Flower.* 1923–4. New York, Museum of Modern Art

10. *The Teetering Woman*. 1923. Düsseldorf, Kunstsammlung Nordrhein-Westfalen

11. *Men Shall Know Nothing of This.* 1923. London, Tate Gallery

12. *At the First Clear Word*. 1923. Düsseldorf, Kunstsammlung Nordrhein-Westfalen

13. *Two Children are Threatened by a Nightingale.* 1924. New York, Museum of Modern Art

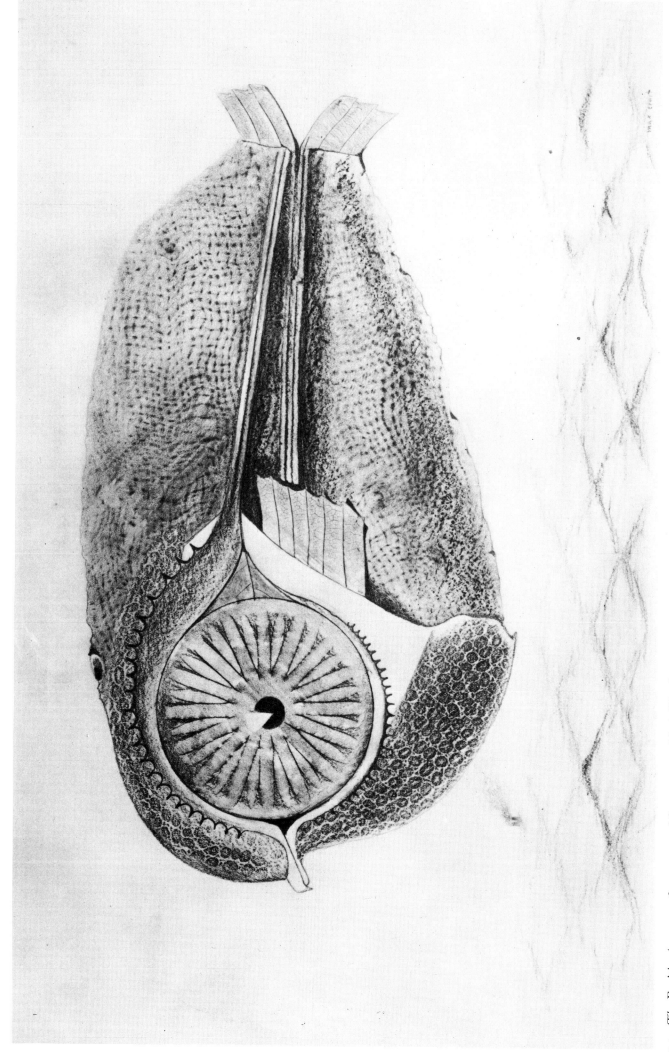

14. *The Fugitive* (no. xxx from a set of frottages entitled *Histoire naturelle*). 1925. Stockholm, Moderna Museet

15. *Yachting* (from a collage novel entitled *La Femme 100 têtes*). 1929. Paris, collection of Natalie de Noailles

16. *Who is this tall, sick man . . .* 1923/4. Switzerland, private collection

17. *Monument to the Birds*. 1927. Paris, private collection

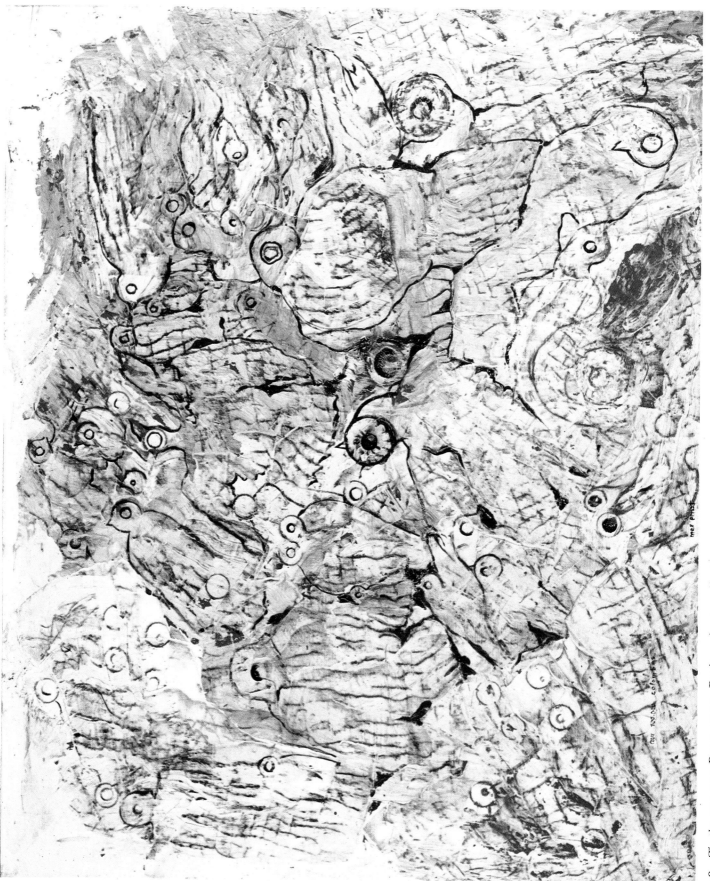

18. *To the 100,000 Doves*. 1925. Paris, private collection

19. *Blue and Pink Doves.* 1926. Düsseldorf, Kunstmuseum

20. *Two Sisters*. 1926. U.S.A., private collection

21. *On the Inside of Sight: The Egg.* 1929. U.S.A., private collection

22. *Snow Flowers*. 1929. Belgium, private collection

23. *Cheval the Postman*. 1929–30. New York, Solomon R. Guggenheim Museum

24. *The Horde.* 1927. Amsterdam, Stedelijk Museum

25. *The Great Forest.* 1927. Basle, Kunstmuseum

26. *One Night of Love*. 1927. Paris, private collection

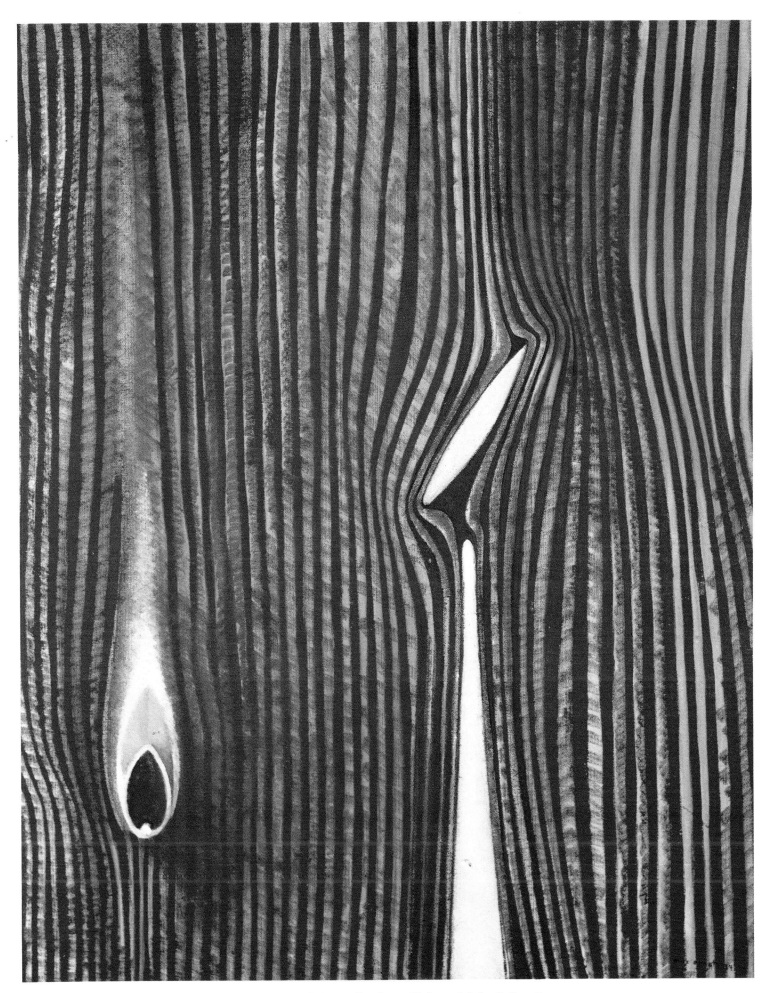

27. *Blind Swimmer: the Effect of Contact.* 1934. U.S.A., collection of Mr and Mrs Julien Levy

28. *Loplop Presents*. 1931. London, private collection

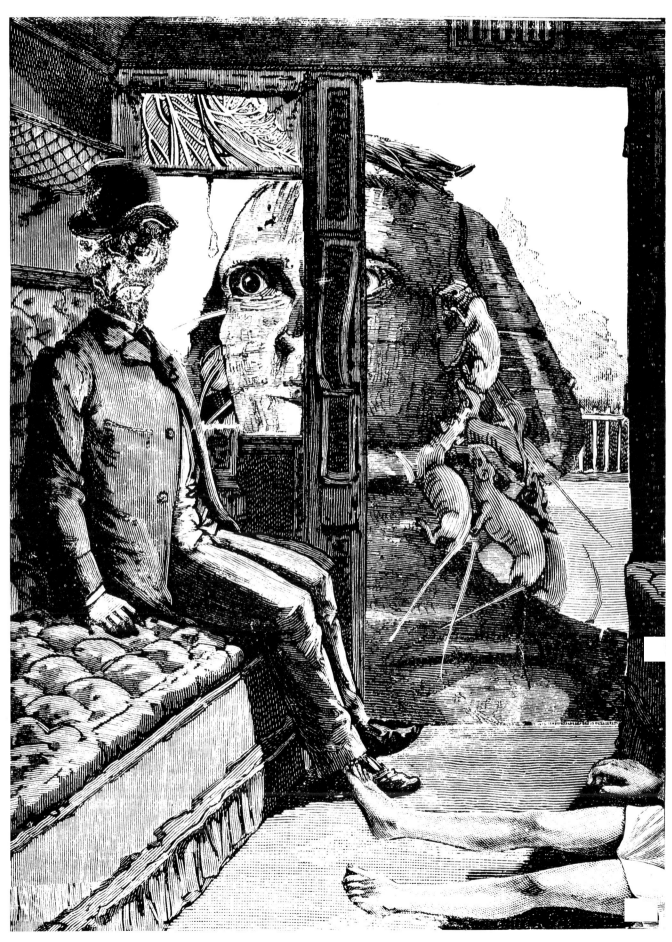

29. *Oedipus* (from a collage novel entitled *Une Semaine de bonté*). 1934

30. *Garden Aeroplane-Trap*. 1935. Paris, Centre Georges Pompidou, Musée National d'Art Moderne

31. *The Whole City.* 1935/6. Zurich, Kunsthaus

34. *The Robing of the Bride*. 1939. Venice, collection of Peggy Guggenheim

35. *Napoleon in the Wilderness*. 1941. New York, Museum of Modern Art

36. *Europe after the Rain II.* 1940–42. Hartford, Connecticut, Wadsworth Atheneum

37. *Vox Angelica*. 1943. New York, Acquavella Galleries

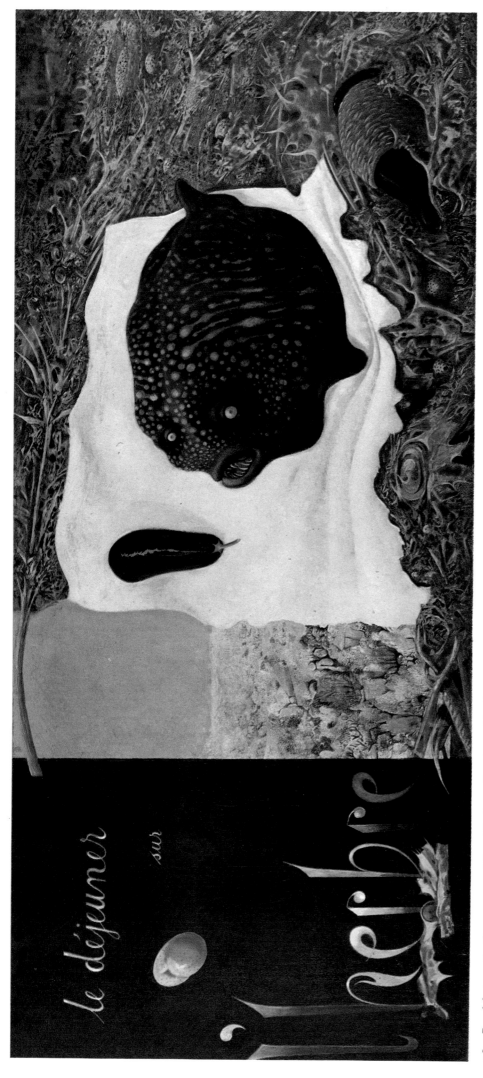

38. *Breakfast on the Grass.* 1944. New York, collection of William N. Copley

39. *The Temptation of St Antony.* 1945. Duisburg, Wilhelm Lehmbruck Museum

40. *Head-Bird*. 1934–5. U.S.A., private collection

41. *The King Playing with the Queen*. 1944. New York, Museum of Modern Art

42. *Young Man Intrigued by the Flight of a Non-Euclidean Fly*. 1942–7. Switzerland, private collection

43. *After Me, Sleep.* 1958. Paris, Centre Georges Pompidou, Musée National d'Art Moderne

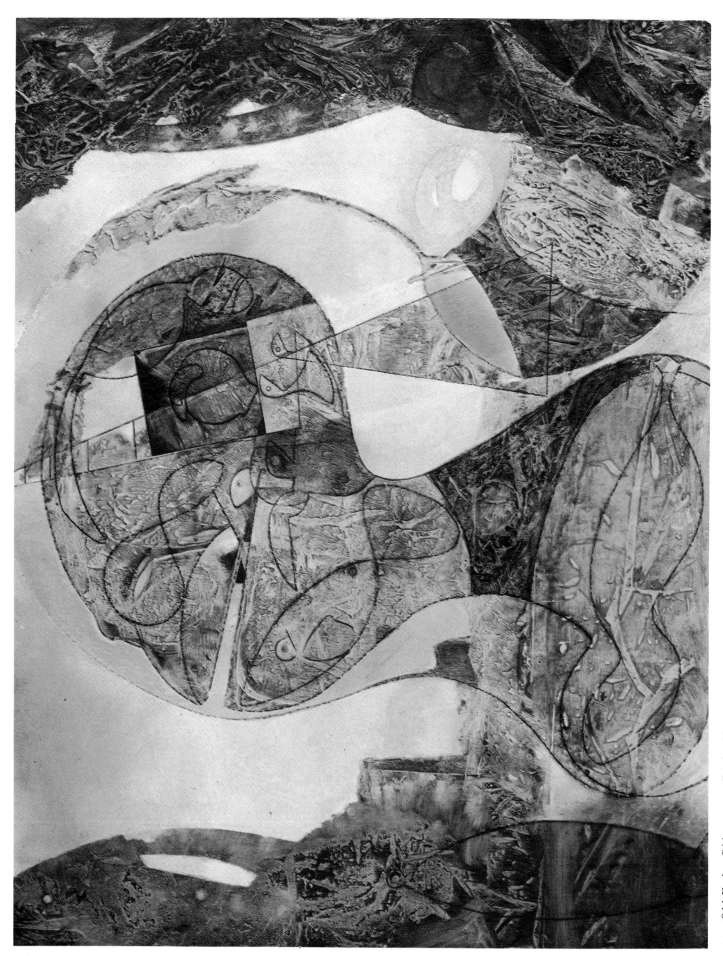

44. *Old Father Rhine*. 1953. Basle, Kunstmuseum

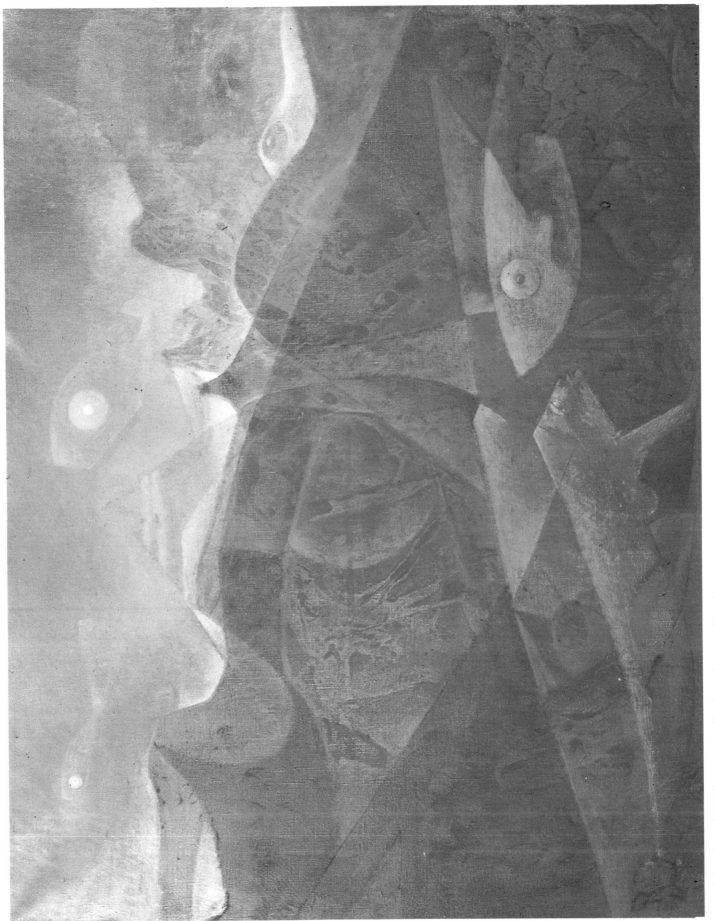

45. *Coloradeau of Medusa*. 1953. Paris, private collection

46. *Almost-Dead Romanticism.* 1960. Milan, private collection

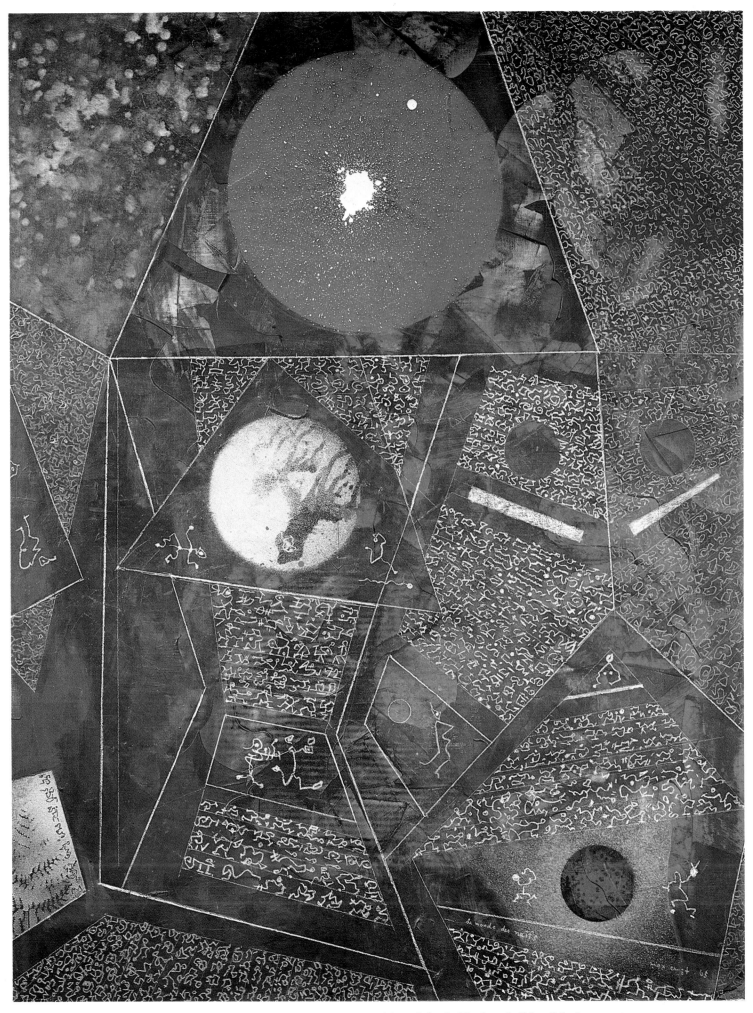

47. *The World of the Naïve*. 1965. Paris, Centre Georges Pompidou, Musée National d'Art Moderne

48. *The Marriage of Heaven and Earth.* 1962. Paris, collection of Lois and Georges de Ménil